Twenty to Make

Mini Christmas Crochet

Val Pierce

First published in Great Britain 2011

Search Press Limited
Wellwood, North Farm Road,
Tunbridge Wells, Kent TN2 3DR

Text copyright © Val Pierce 2011

Photographs by Paul Bricknell at
Search Press Studios

Photographs and design copyright
© Search Press Ltd 2011

ISBN 978 1 84448 740 0

Suppliers

If you have difficulty in obtaining any of the
materials and equipment mentioned in this book
then please visit the Search Press website for
details of suppliers: www.searchpress.com

Printed in Spain

Dedication
I dedicate this book to Abi, Ellie,
Oliver, Ryan and Aimee. You all add
extra sparkle to every Christmas by
being the special little people you are!

Contents

Introduction

'Christmas comes but once a year and when it does it brings good cheer', so why not bring your very own cheer to this magical time of year by creating some or all of the delightful little crocheted decorations I have designed for this book.

There is nothing quite like making your own tree hangings, either for yourself or to give as a special gift to a close friend or relative. They can be packed away and used year after year and even handed down through the generations, giving you and your family pleasure for many years to come. Some of the pieces are free-standing, but there is no reason why you shouldn't add hanging loops and use them to adorn your Christmas tree too.

My favourite colours are reds, golds and greens, but all the items can be crocheted in whatever yarns or colours you want to match your particular Christmas theme, whether it be traditional, cool and trendy, or simple and childlike.

All of the designs can be made quickly and easily using scraps and oddments of yarn, so even those new to crochet will be able to make an impressive collection of novelty knits for the festive season. Add a tiny gift inside the cracker, or use it instead of a place card at the Christmas dinner table; use sparkly yarns, beads and sequins, or even embroider on a name to make these novelty knits truly your very own creation. Whatever you decide to do I am sure that you will have as much fun making them as I did designing them. Happy Christmas crocheting!

Here is a selection of the mini crocheted Christmas decorations you can make using the patterns in this book. In a range of colours and styles that can easily be adapted to suit your personal taste, they make perfect little projects for the festive season.

American and British crochet terminology

In all the patterns, US terms are given first, followed by the UK terms afterwards in brackets. So US single crochet would be written as sc (*UKdc*) and US double crochet as dc (*UKtr*).

The most frequently used terms are:

American	British
slip stitch (sl st)	slip stitch (sl st)
chain stitch (ch)	chain stitch (ch)
single crochet (sc)	double crochet (dc)
half double crochet (hdc)	half treble crochet (htr)
double crochet (dc)	treble crochet (tr)
treble crochet (tr)	double treble crochet (dtr)
double treble crochet (dtr)	triple treble crochet (trtr)
skip	miss

Materials

All the decorations are made using a size 2.00mm (US B-1, UK 14) crochet hook, though for the Christmas Bear you will also need a 4.00mm (US G-6, UK 8) crochet hook. Either a no. 5 or no. 3 crochet cotton is used throughout, though if you prefer a fine 4-ply yarn can be used instead. Most of the items use only small amounts of yarn, making them ideal for using up scraps and oddments.

You will also need various embellishments, including bows, stars, ribbons, buttons and beads; a sewing needle and thread; craft glue; and toy stuffing.

Measurements

Approximate measurements of all the pieces are provided, but remember that if you use different yarns from those specified, the finished sizes may vary.

Techniques

Some of the decorations are worked in the round, which is sometimes a little difficult to master, so always place a marker at the beginning of the round so that you know where you started; it is very easy to end up with either too many or too few stitches if you don't know where the row began.

One or two of the designs are stuffed as you make them, and again this is a technique that you will need to get used to. It does make it a little difficult to crochet sometimes, especially when the opening is quite small. The secret is to add only tiny bits of stuffing at a time.

This magical little tree is perfect for adorning the Christmas dinner table (see pattern on page 38). Make one for every guest at your festive gathering – a wonderful little keepsake for them to take home and treasure!

Pine Cones

Materials and equipment:

Crochet hook size 2.00mm (US B-1, UK 14)

Gold metallic yarn – 1 ball

Holly berry embellishment

0.5m (20in) of narrow gold ribbon

Toy stuffing

Craft glue

Sewing needle and gold thread (optional)

Measurements:

The pine cone is approximately 5cm (2in) high.

Special abbreviations:

3dc (UKtr) cluster – draw up loop, yrh, hook into space, draw up loop, repeat 3 times, yrh, draw through all loops, 1 ch to secure.
4dc (UKtr) cluster – as above but repeat 4 times.

Instructions:

Using gold metallic yarn, make 6 ch then join with sl st into a ring.
Round 1: work 12 sc (UKdc) into the ring then join with a sl st.
Round 2: work a 3dc (UKtr) cluster into each sc (UKdc), join with a sl st to top of first 3dc (UKtr) cluster [12 3dc (UKtr) clusters].
Round 3: sl st into first space between clusters, work 3dc (UKtr) cluster, 1 ch into each space, join with a sl st to top of first 3dc (UKtr) cluster.
Round 4: sl st into next 2 ch sp, work *4dc (UKtr) cluster, 1 ch* into each 2 ch sp, join with a sl st to top of first 4dc (UKtr) cluster.
Round 5: repeat round 4.
Round 6: sl st into next 2 ch sp, *3dc (UKtr) cluster, 1 sc (UKdc)* into each 2 ch sp, join with a sl st to top of 3dc (UKtr) cluster.
Round 7: sl st into next 2 ch sp, 3dc (UKtr) cluster into each 1 ch sp, but omit the 1 ch to secure, join as previous round.

To make up

Carefully push tiny pieces of stuffing inside the pine cone using the crochet hook to help you. Do not overstuff – just get a pleasing shape. Using a small amount of craft glue, attach the holly berry embellishment to the top of the pine cone. Thread ribbon through the last row of clusters. Decide how long you want the ribbon loop to be and trim the ribbon as necessary. Either tie the ends of the ribbon together in a knot or stitch them to form a loop.

Festive Wreath

Materials and equipment:

Crochet hook size 2.00mm (US B-1, UK 14)

No. 5 crochet cotton – 1 ball of dark green, 1 ball of light green

3 small holly berry embellishments

0.5m (20in) of narrow green satin ribbon

Gold ribbon bow or a short length of gold ribbon to tie in a bow

Gold bell

Craft glue

Sewing needle and green thread (optional)

Measurements:

The wreath is approximately 7cm (2¾in) in diameter.

Instructions:

Using light green crochet cotton, make 50 ch. Row 1: Work 2 dc (*UKtr*) into 3rd ch from hook, 3 dc (*UKtr*) into each ch to end. As you work, the crochet will twirl into a tight corkscrew shape.

Use dark green cotton to make another twist in the same way.

To make up

Secure both the light green and dark green crochet twists together at one end, then twine the strips around each other, folding the coils inside one another as you do so, until you get a neat double coil. Join the two ends together firmly.

Glue the holy berry embellishments on the coil at random, tucking them inside the twists. Glue the ribbon bow and bell at the top of the wreath to cover the join where the ends of the twists meet.

Thread the ribbon through the top of the wreath to make a hanging loop. Decide how long you want the ribbon loop to be and trim the ribbon as necessary. Either tie the ends of the ribbon together in a knot or stitch them to form a loop.

Dove of Peace

Materials and equipment:

Crochet hook size 2.00mm (US B-1, UK 14)

No. 3 crochet cotton – 1 ball of pale lilac, 1 ball of pale blue and small amounts of yellow and black

Small amount of gold metallic yarn

Gold ribbon rose

0.5m (20in) of narrow lilac ribbon

Needle and lilac thread

Small amount of stuffing

Measurements:

The dove is approximately 6cm (2¼in) high and 9cm (3½in) long.

Instructions:

Head

Using lilac crochet cotton, make 2 ch.
Round 1: work 6 sc (UKdc) into 2nd ch from hook then join with a sl st to form a tight circle.
Round 2: 2 sc (UKdc) into each st around [12 sts].
Round 3: *1 sc (UKdc) into next sc (UKdc), 2 sc (UKdc) into next sc (UKdc),* repeat from * to * all around [18 sts].
Round 4: *1 sc (UKdc) into each of next 2 sc (UKdc), 2 sc (UKdc) into next sc (UKdc),* repeat from * to * all around [24 sts].
Rounds 5–9: work in sc (UKdc) all around.
You will now begin decreasing. Stuff the head before you close it up.
Round 10: *1 sc (UKdc) into each of next 2 sc (UKdc), sc (UKdc) 2 tog,* repeat from * to * all around.
Round 11: work in sc (UKdc) all around.
Round 12: *1 sc (UKdc) in next sc (UKdc), sc (UKdc) 2 tog,* repeat from * to * all around.
Round 13: work in sc (UKdc) all around.
Round 14: sc (UKdc) 2 tog all around, join with a sl st. Fasten off.

Body

Using lilac crochet cotton, make 2 ch.
Round 1: work 6 sc (UKdc) into 2nd ch from hook then join with a sl st to form a tight circle.
Round 2: 2 sc (UKdc) into each sc (UKdc) around [12 sts].
Round 3: *1 sc (UKdc) into next sc (UKdc), 2 sc (UKdc) into next sc (UKdc),* repeat from * to * all around [18 sts].
Round 4: *1 sc (UKdc) into each of next 2 sc (UKdc), 2 sc (UKdc) into next sc (UKdc),* repeat from * to * all around [24 sts].
Round 5: * 1 sc (UKdc) into each of next 3 sc (UKdc), 2 sc (UKdc) into next sc (UKdc),* repeat from * to * all around [30 sts].
Rounds 6–12: work in sc (UKdc) all around.
You will now begin decreasing. Stuff the body before you close it up.
Round: 13: *1 sc (UKdc) into each of next 3 sc (UKdc), sc (UKdc) 2 tog,* repeat from * to * all around.
Rounds 14–16: work in sc (UKdc) all around.
Round 17: *1 sc (UKdc) into each of next 2 sc (UKdc), sc (UKdc) 2 tog,* repeat from * to * all around.
Rounds 18–20: work in sc (UKdc) all.around.
Round 21: *1 sc (UKdc) into next sc (UKdc), sc (UKdc) 2 tog,* repeat from * to * all around.
Rounds 22–23: work in sc (UKdc) all around.
Round 24: sc (UKdc) 2 tog all around.
Rounds 25–26: work in sc (UKdc). Fasten off. This is the tail end.

Wings

Using blue crochet cotton, make 8 ch then join with a sl st into ring.

Round 1: 7 ch to count as 1 dtr (UKtrtr) and 2 ch, *1 dtr (UKtrtr) 2 ch into ring,* repeat from * to * 14 times more then join with a sl st to 5th ch of starting ch [sixteen 2 ch sp].

Round 2: 2 ch, 2 sc (UKdc) into first 2 ch sp, *3 sc (UKdc) into next 2 ch sp,* repeat all around and join with a sl st to beg [48 sts].

Round 3: 8 ch for first sc (UKdc) and 7 ch loop, 1 sc (UKdc) into 3rd sc (UKdc), *5 ch, miss 2 sc (UKdc), 1 sc (UKdc) into next sc (UKdc), 7 ch, miss 2 sc (UKdc), 1 sc (UKdc) into next sc (UKdc),* repeat from * to * all around, ending last repeat 5 ch, join with sl st to beg.

Round 4: sl st into first 7 ch loop, into loop work 3 ch, 4 dc (UKtr), 4 ch, sl st into 3rd ch from hook (1 picot made), 1 ch, 5 dc (UKtr) into loop, *1 sc (UKdc) into next 5 ch loop, [5dc (UKtr), 4 ch, sl st into 3rd ch from hook (1 picot made), 5 dc (UKtr)] all into next 7 ch loop,* repeat from * to * all around, join with a sl st to beg. Fasten off.

Round 5: join in gold to any point and work 1 row of sc (UKdc) all around, join with a sl st and fasten off.

Beak

Using yellow crochet cotton, make 7 ch. Work 1 sc (UKdc) into 2nd ch from hook, 1 sc (UKdc) into each ch to end. Fasten off.

To make up

Sew the head to the body at a slight angle. Embroider the eyes on the head, then fold the beak in half lengthways and stitch in position on the head. Fold the wings in half, matching the points, then stitch them to the centre of the back. Glue the ribbon rose on top.

Thread the lilac ribbon through the top of the body to make a hanging loop. Decide how long you want the ribbon loop to be and trim the ribbon as necessary. Either tie the ends of the ribbon together in a knot or stitch them to form a loop.

13

Glimmering Snowflake

Materials and equipment:

Crochet hook size 2.00mm (US B-1, UK 14)

No. 5 crochet cotton – 1 ball of white (this is sufficient for several snowflakes)

8 pearl beads

1 large pearlised snowflake button

0.5m (20in) of narrow white ribbon

Sewing needle and white thread

Measurements:

The snowflake is approximately 9cm (3½in) in diameter.

Instructions (make 2):

Using white crochet cotton, make 8 ch then join with sl st into a ring.

Round 1: 7 ch to count as 1 dtr (UKtrtr) and 2 ch, *1 dtr (UKtrtr) 2 ch into the ring,* repeat from * to * 14 times more, then join with a sl st into 5th ch of starting ch [sixteen 2ch sp].

Round 2: 2 ch, 2 sc (UKdc) into first 2ch sp, *3 sc (UKdc) into next 2ch sp,* repeat all around and join with a sl st to beg [48 sts].

Round 3: 8 ch, for first sc (UKdc) and 7 ch loop, 1 sc (UKdc) into 3rd sc (UKdc), *5 ch, miss 2 sc (UKdc), 1 sc (UKdc) into next sc (UKdc), 7 ch, miss 2 sc (UKdc), 1 sc (UKdc) into next sc (UKdc),* repeat from * to * all around, ending last repeat 5 ch, join with sl st to beg.

Round 4: sl st into first 7 ch loop, into loop work 3 ch, 4 dc (UKtr), 4 ch, sl st into 3rd ch from hook (1 picot made), 1 ch, 5 dc (UKtr) into loop, *1 sc (UKdc) into next 5 ch loop, [5 dc (UKtr), 4 ch, sl st into 3rd ch from hook (1 picot made), 5 dc (UKtr)] all into next 7 ch loop,* repeat from * to * all around, join with a sl st to beg. Fasten off.

To make up

Place the two snowflakes back to back and sew them together neatly, matching the points as you do so. Sew the large snowflake button to the centre of the snowflake and then sew a small pearl to the centre of each point, using the photograph as a guide.

Thread the ribbon through the top of one point to make a hanging loop. Decide how long you want the ribbon loop to be and trim the ribbon as necessary. Either tie the ends of the ribbon together in a knot or stitch them to form a loop.

Tip

You can spray starch on to the snowflake before attaching the button and beads to give it a firmer texture.

Christmas Stocking

Materials and equipment:

Crochet hook size 2.00mm (US B-1, UK 14)

No. 3 crochet cotton – 1 ball of red and a small amount of white

4 snowflake buttons (8 if you wish to embellish both sides)

Silver ribbon bow

0.5m (20in) of narrow silver ribbon

Sewing needle and thread to match the buttons and ribbon

Measurements:

The Christmas stocking is approximately 10cm (4in) high.

Instructions:

Using white crochet cotton, make 29 ch.
Row 1: 1 sc (*UKdc*) into 2nd ch from hook, 1 sc (*UKdc*) into each ch to end; turn [28 sts].
Rows 2–3: work 1 sc (*UKdc*) into each sc (*UKdc*) to end.
Row 4: join in red. *Insert hook into first sc (*UKdc*) and pull yarn through, then insert hook into corresponding sc (*UKdc*) 2 rows below, draw up loop and work as normal sc (*UKdc*),* repeat to end.
Row 5: using red, work 1 row in sc (*UKdc*).
Row 6: using white, work 1 row in sc (*UKdc*).
Row 7: using white, repeat row 4.
Row 8: using white, work 1 row in sc (*UKdc*).
Rows 9–20: using red, work each st in sc (*UKdc*).

Now create the top of the foot:
Row 1: work in sc (*UKdc*) across 18 sts, turn.
Row 2: work in sc (*UKdc*) across 8 sts, turn.
Rows 3–10: work in sc (*UKdc*) on these 8 sts. Break yarn.

Work foot as follows:
Rejoin yarn and work 10 sc (*UKdc*) along the right side of the top of the foot, 8 sc (*UKdc*) across the toe, and 10 sc (*UKdc*) down the left side of top of foot then finally work across the remaining 10 sc (*UKdc*) of the foot [48 sts], turn.

Rows 1–6: work in sc (*UKdc*) across all sts.
Row 7: sc (*UKdc*) 2 tog, sc (*UKdc*) 20, sc (*UKdc*) 2 tog twice, sc (*UKdc*) 20, sc (*UKdc*) 2 tog.
Row 8: sc (*UKdc*) 2 tog, sc (*UKdc*) 18, sc (*UKdc*) 2 tog twice, sc (*UKdc*) 18, sc (*UKdc*) 2 tog.
Row 9: sc (*UKdc*) 2 tog, sc (*UKdc*) 16, sc (*UKdc*) 2 tog twice, sc (*UKdc*) 16, sc (*UKdc*) 2 tog.
Row 10: sc (*UKdc*) 2 tog, sc (*UKdc*) 14, sc (*UKdc*) 2 tog twice, sc (*UKdc*) 14, sc (*UKdc*) 2 tog.
Row 11: sc (*UKdc*) 2 tog, work in sc (*UKdc*) to last 2 sts, sc (*UKdc*) 2 tog; fasten off.

To make up

Work in the yarn ends and sew the foot and back seam of the stocking. Attach the snowflake buttons and the ribbon bow, using the photograph as a guide. Fold the silver ribbon in half to make a hanging loop, trimming it to the required length, and attach it to the stocking.

Rudolf the Reindeer

Materials and equipment:

Crochet hook size 2.00mm (US B-1, UK 14)

No. 5 crochet cotton – 1 ball of mid brown and 1 ball of dark brown

Oddment of red metallic yarn

Black embroidery floss or oddment of black crochet cotton

Tiny gold bow and bell embellishment

Small amount of stuffing

Sewing needle and threads to match the yarns

Measurements:

Rudolf is approximately 10cm (4in) high to the top of his head.

Instructions:

Body

Using mid brown crochet cotton, make 2 sc (UKdc).

Round 1: work 6 sc (UKdc) into 2nd ch from hook then join with a sl st to form a tight circle.

Round 2: work 2 sc (UKdc) into each st around [12 sts].

Round 3: *1 sc (UKdc) into next sc (UKdc), 2 sc (UKdc) into next sc (UKdc),* repeat from * to * all around [18 sts].

Round 4: *1 sc (UKdc) into each of next 2 sc (UKdc), 2 sc (UKdc) into next sc (UKdc),* repeat from * to * all around [24 sts].

Round 5: *1 sc (UKdc) into each of next 3 sc (UKdc), 2 sc (UKdc) into next sc (UKdc),* repeat from * to * all around [30 sts].

Rounds 6–16: work in sc (UKdc) all around. You will now begin decreasing. Stuff the body as you work.

Round 17: *1 sc (UKdc) into each of next 3 sc (UKdc), sc (UKdc) 2 tog,* repeat from * to * all around.

Round 18: *1 sc (UKdc) into each of next 2 sc (UKdc), sc (UKdc) 2 tog,* repeat from * to * all around.

Round 19: work in sc (UKdc) all around.

Round 20: sc (UKdc) 2 tog all around. Break yarn. Finish stuffing the body and then run the yarn through the last row of sts, draw up and fasten off.

Head

Using mid brown crochet cotton, make 2 sc (UKdc).

Round 1: work 6 sc (UKdc) into 2nd ch from hook then join with a sl st to form a tight circle.

Round 2: work 2 sc (UKdc) into each st around [12 sts].

Round 3: *1 sc (UKdc) into next sc (UKdc), 2 sc (UKdc) into next sc (UKdc),* repeat from * to * all around [18 sts].

Rounds 4–7: work in sc (UKdc) all around.

Round 8: *1 sc (UKdc) into each of next 2 sc (UKdc), 2 sc (UKdc) into next sc (UKdc),* repeat from * to * all around then join with a sl st.

Round 9: work in sc (UKdc) all around then join with a sl st.

Round 10: *1 sc (UKdc) into next sc (UKdc), 2 sc (UKdc) into next sc (UKdc),* repeat from * to * all around then join with a sl st as before.
Rounds 11–15: work 1 sc (UKdc) into each sc (UKdc) all around then join with a sl st as before. You will now begin decreasing. Stuff the head as you work.
Round 16: *1 sc (UKdc) in each of next 2 sc (UKdc), sc (UKdc) 2 tog,* repeat from * to * all around then join with a sl st as before.
Round 17: work in sc (UKdc) all around then join with a sl st.
Round 18: *1 sc (UKdc) into next sc (UKdc), sc (UKdc) 2 tog,* repeat from * to * all around then join with a sl st.
Round 19: work in sc (UKdc) all around then join with a sl st.
Round 20: sc (UKdc) 2 tog all around then join with a sl st. Fasten off.
Finish stuffing the head, if needed, then run the yarn through the last row of sts and draw up tight. Fasten off.

Front legs (make 2)
Using mid brown crochet cotton, make 6 ch.
Row 1: 1 sc (UKdc) into 2nd ch from hook, 1 sc (UKdc) into each ch to end, turn.
Rows 2–3: work in sc (UKdc), increasing 1 sc (UKdc) at each end of row.
Work 4 rows in sc (UKdc).
Break mid brown and join in dark brown.
Work 2 rows in sc (UKdc).
Next row: work in sc (UKdc), increasing 1 sc (UKdc) at each end of row.
Next row: work in sc (UKdc). Fasten off.

Back legs (make 2)
Using mid brown crochet cotton, make 10 ch.
Row 1: 1 sc (UKdc) into 2nd ch from hook, 1 sc (UKdc) into each ch to end, turn.
Row 2: 1 ch, 1 sc (UKdc) into each sc (UKdc) to end, turn.
Rows 3–4: work in sc (UKdc), increasing 1 sc (UKdc) at each end of row.
Work 8 rows in sc (UKdc).
Change to dark brown and work 4 rows in sc (UKdc).
Next row: work in sc (UKdc), decreasing 1 sc (UKdc) at each end of row.
Next row: repeat previous row. Fasten off.

Large antlers (make 2)
Using dark brown crochet cotton, make 12 ch.
Row 1: 1 sc (UKdc) into 2nd ch from hook, 1 sc (UKdc) into each ch to end, turn.
Rows 2–4: 1 ch, 1 sc (UKdc) into each sc (UKdc) to end, turn.
Fasten off.

Small antlers (make 2)
Using dark brown crochet cotton, make 6 ch.
Row 1: 1 sc (UKdc) into 2nd ch from hook, 1 sc (UKdc) into each ch to end, turn.
Rows 2–4: 1 ch, 1 sc (UKdc) into each sc (UKdc) to end, turn.
Fasten off.

Ears (make 2)
Using mid brown crochet cotton, make 2 ch.
Row 1: work 1 sc (UKdc) into 2nd ch from hook.
Row 2: 1 ch, 3 sc (UKdc) into next sc (UKdc), turn.
Rows 3–4: 1 ch, 1 sc (UKdc) into each sc (UKdc) to end, turn.
Row 5: 1 ch, sc (UKdc) 2 tog, 1 sc (UKdc) in last sc (UKdc), turn.
Row 6: sc (UKdc) 2 tog. Fasten off.

Nose
Using red metallic yarn, make 2 ch. Work 14 dc (UKtr) into 2nd ch from hook then join with a sl st to first dc (UKtr) worked. Fasten off.

To make up
Work in all the ends. Attach the red nose to the head. With black cotton embroider the eyes with French knots and use straight stitches for the mouth. Sew the ears on to each side of the head, using the photograph as a guide. Fold each antler in half lengthways and stitch along the side seam. Sew a short antler on to each long antler at a slight angle, using the photograph as a guide if needed. Now sew the antlers to the head just above the ears. Sew the head on to the body.

Fold the front legs in half lengthways and sew the side seams. Stuff lightly, adding extra at the hoof (dark brown) end to pad them out a little. Oversew a length of cotton through the centre of the hoof end to create the cloven effect. Make up the back legs in the same way. Attach the legs to the body, remembering that Rudolf is sitting down.

Good Fairy

Materials and equipment:

Crochet hook size 2.00mm (US B-1, UK 14)

No. 3 crochet cotton – 1 ball of pale pink, 1 ball of deep pink and small amounts of blue and red for the features

Small amount of gold metallic yarn

2 gold ribbon bows

2 tiny gold self-adhesive craft stars

0.5m (20in) narrow pink ribbon

Cocktail stick

Small piece of gold cushion piping

Sewing needles and thread to match the yarns

Small amount of stuffing

Craft glue

Measurements:

The fairy is approximately 10cm (4in) tall.

Instructions:

Head

Using pale pink crochet cotton, make 2 ch.
Round 1: work 6 sc (*UKdc*) into 2nd ch from hook then join with a sl st to form a tight circle.
Round 2: work 2 sc (*UKdc*) into eachst around [12 sts].
Round 3: *1 sc (*UKdc*) into next sc (*UKdc*), 2 sc (*UKdc*) into next sc (*UKdc*),* repeat from * to * all around [18 sts].
Round 4: *1 sc (*UKdc*) into each of next 2 sc (*UKdc*), 2 sc (*UKdc*) in next sc (*UKdc*),* repeat from * to * all around [24 sts].
Rounds 5–9: work in sc (*UKdc*) all around.
You will now begin decreasing. Stuff the head before you close it up.
Round 10: *1 sc (*UKdc*) into each of next 2 sc (*UKdc*), sc (*UKdc*) 2 tog,* repeat from * to * all around.
Round 11: work in sc (*UKdc*) all around.
Round 12: *1 sc (*UKdc*) into next sc (*UKdc*), sc (*UKdc*) 2 tog,* repeat from * to * all around.
Round 13: work in sc (*UKdc*) all around.
Round 14: sc (*UKdc*) 2 tog all around then join with a sl st. Fasten off.

Body

Using pale pink crochet cotton, make 2 sc (*UKdc*).
Round 1: work 6 sc (*UKdc*) into 2nd ch from hook then join with a sl st to form a tight circle.
Round 2: 2 sc (*UKdc*) into each st around [12 sts].
Round 3: *1 sc (*UKdc*) into next sc (*UKdc*), 2 sc (*UKdc*) into next sc (*UKdc*),* repeat from * to * all around [18 sts].
Round 4: *1 sc (*UKdc*) into each of next 2 sc (*UKdc*), 2 sc (*UKdc*) into next sc (*UKdc*),* repeat from * to * all around [24 sts].
Round 5: *1 sc (*UKdc*) into each of next 3 sc (*UKdc*), 2 sc (*UKdc*) into next sc (*UKdc*),* repeat from * to * all around [30 sts].
Rounds 6–14: work in sc (*UKdc*) all around. Fasten off.

Base

Using pale pink crochet cotton, work as body up to end of round 3.

Dress (worked from neck down)

Using dark pink crochet cotton, make 10 ch then join with sl st into a ring.

Round 1: into the ring work 2 ch, 15 sc (UKdc) then join with a sl st [16 sc (UKdc)].

Round 2: 2 ch, 1 dc (UKtr) into same st, 2 dc (UKtr) into each sc (UKdc) to end, join with a sl st [32 dc (UKtr)].

Round 3: 2 ch, 1 dc (UKtr) in same st, 2 dc (UKtr) into each of next 5 dc (UKtr), 4 ch, miss next 4 ch, 2 dc (UKtr) into each of next 12 dc (UKtr), 4 ch, miss next 4 ch, 2 dc (UKtr) into remaining 6 dc (UKtr), join with a sl st.

Round 4: *3 ch, miss 1 dc (UKtr), sc (UKdc) into next dc (UKtr) or st,* repeat from * to * all around, do not join.

Round 5: *3 ch, 1 sc (UKdc) into 3 ch loop of previous round,* repeat from * to * all around. Continue as last row until you have eight 3 ch loop rows in all.

Next round: *3 dc (UKtr), 3 ch, 3 dc (UKtr) into next 3 ch loop, 1 sc (UKdc) into next 3 ch loop,* repeat from * to * all around, ending with 3 dc (UKtr), 3 ch, 3 dc (UKtr), sl st to beg of round.

Next round: join in gold yarn and work 1 sc (UKdc) into each st around the base of the skirt.

Arms (make 2)

Using pale pink crochet cotton, make 10 ch.

Row 1: 1 sc (UKdc) into 2nd ch from hook, 1 sc (UKdc) into each ch to end, turn.

Rows 2–4: 1 ch, 1 sc (UKdc) into each sc (UKdc) to end, turn. Fasten off.

Wings (make 2)

Using deep pink crochet cotton, make 2 ch.

Row 1: work 5 dc (UKtr) into 2nd ch from hook, turn.

Row 2: 3 ch, 1 dc (UKtr) into first st, 2 dc (UKtr) into each st to end, turn.

Row 3: join in gold yarn and work 1 sc (UKdc) into each st to end, turn.

Row 4: work 2 sc (UKdc) into each sc (UKdc) to end. Fasten off.

Wand

Take the cocktail stick and wind gold yarn tightly around it. Secure the ends with some craft glue. Stick the two craft stars together with the cocktail stick sandwiched in between them.

To make up

Sew in any loose ends on all pieces. Stuff the body and attach the base. Invert the base a little to enable the fairy to stand up. Place the body inside the dress, thread ribbon through the waist of the dress and tie it firmly to hold the body inside, adding a few stitches if needed; trim the ends. Sew the gold ribbon bow on to the front of the dress.

Fold each arm in half lengthways and stitch the sides. Position an arm on each side of the fairy, pushing it through the armhole of the dress. Sew these in place. Place the wand into one hand and glue in place. Sew the wings together in the centre and stitch these to the back of the fairy.

Unwind the strands of the gold cushion piping using a needle to tease the strands out into ringlets. Cut the strands into equal lengths and glue them to the top of the fairy's head; trim them to a nice shape. Sew a tiny gold bow to the top of the head. Embroider the features. Finally, attach the head to the body.

Baby Penguin

Materials and equipment:

Crochet hook size 2.00mm (US B-1, UK 14) *2mm*

No. 3 crochet cotton – 1 ball of white and 1 ball of black

Small amounts of yellow, blue and silver metallic yarn

Sewing needle and threads to match the yarn

Small amount of stuffing

Measurements:

The penguin is approximately 8.5cm (3in) tall, including his hat.

Instructions:

Using white crochet cotton, make 2 ch, work 6 sc (*UKdc*) into 2nd ch from hook then join with sl st into a ring.

Round 1: work 2 sc (*UKdc*) into each sc (*UKdc*) to end then join with a sl st.

Round 2: *1 sc (*UKdc*) into next sc (*UKdc*), 2 sc (*UKdc*) into next sc (*UKdc*),* repeat from * to * all around then join with a sl st as before.

Round 3: *1 sc (*UKdc*) into each of next 2 sc (*UKdc*), 2 sc (*UKdc*) into next sc (*UKdc*),* repeat from * to * all around then join with a sl st as before.

Round 4: *1 sc (*UKdc*) into each of next 3 sc (*UKdc*), 2 sc (*UKdc*) into next sc (*UKdc*),* repeat from * to * all around then join with a sl st as before.

Round 5: 1 sc (*UKdc*) into each of next 4 sc (*UKdc*), 2 sc (*UKdc*) into next sc (*UKdc*),* repeat from * to * all around then join with a sl st as before.

Work 4 rounds in sc (*UKdc*) with no increase. Change to black and work 4 rounds of sc (*UKdc*).

Now shape the top, stuffing the penguin as you go.

Next round: *1 sc (*UKdc*) into each of next 4 sc (*UKdc*), sc (*UKdc*) 2 tog,* repeat from * to * all around then join with a sl st as before.

Next round: *1 sc (*UKdc*) into each of next 3 sc (*UKdc*), sc (*UKdc*) 2 tog,* repeat from * to * all around then join with a sl st as before.

Next round: *1 sc (*UKdc*) into each of next 2 sc (*UKdc*), sc (*UKdc*) 2 tog,* repeat from * to * all around then join with a sl st as before.

Next round: *1 sc (*UKdc*) into next sc (*UKdc*), sc (*UKdc*) 2 tog,* repeat from * to * all around then join with a sl st as before.

Next round: sc (*UKdc*) 2 tog all around. Fasten off and run thread through the last row of sts; draw up and fasten off.

Feet (make 2)

Using yellow, make 7 ch.

Row 1: 1 sc (*UKdc*) into 2nd ch from hook, 1 sc (*UKdc*) into each ch to end, turn [6 sts].

Row 2: 1 ch, work 1 sc (*UKdc*) into each sc (*UKdc*) to end, turn.

Rows 3–4: work in sc (*UKdc*), decreasing 1 sc (*UKdc*) at each end of row.

Rows 5–6: work in sc (*UKdc*) on these 2 sts.

Rows 7–8: work in sc (*UKdc*), increasing 1 sc (*UKdc*) at each end of row.

Work 2 rows in sc (*UKdc*) on these 6 sts then fasten off.

Beak
Using yellow, make 7 ch.
Row 1: 1 sc (*UKdc*) into 2nd ch from hook, 1 sc (*UKdc*) into each ch to end, turn [6 sts].
Rows 2–3: work in sc (*UKdc*), decreasing 1 sc (*UKdc*) at each end of row.
Rows 4–5: work in sc (*UKdc*) on these 2 sts.
Rows 6–7: work in sc (*UKdc*), increasing 1 sc (*UKdc*) at each end of row.
Work 1 row in sc (*UKdc*) on these 6 sts then fasten off.

Wings (make 2)
Using black, make 2 ch.
Row 1: 2 sc (*UKdc*) into 2nd ch from hook, turn.
Row 2: 2 sc (*UKdc*) into first sc (*UKdc*), 1 sc (*UKdc*) into next sc (*UKdc*), turn.
Row 3: 2 sc (*UKdc*) into first sc (*UKdc*), 1 sc (*UKdc*) into next sc (*UKdc*), 2 sc (*UKdc*) into last sc (*UKdc*).
Rows 4–7: work sc (*UKdc*) on these 5 sts.
Rows 8–9: work in sc (*UKdc*), decreasing 1 sc (*UKdc*) at each end of row. Fasten off.

Eyes (make 2)
Using white, make 2 ch, work 6 sc (*UKdc*) into 2nd ch from hook then join with a sl st into a ring.
Round 1: 1 ch, work 2 sc (*UKdc*) into each sc (*UKdc*) all around, join with a sl st.
Round 2: 1 ch, *1 sc (*UKdc*) into next sc (*UKdc*), 2 sc (*UKdc*) into next sc (*UKdc*),* repeat from * to * all around, join with a sl st to beg of round. Fasten off.

Pupils (make 2)
Using black, make 2 ch. Work 6 sc (*UKdc*) into 2nd ch from hook then join with sl st into a circle.

Hat
Using blue, make 21 ch loosely.
Row 1: work 1 dc (*UKtr*) into 3rd ch from hook, 1 dc (*UKtr*) into each ch to end, turn.
Row 2: 3 ch [counts as 1 dc (*UKtr*)], 1 dc (*UKtr*) into each dc (*UKtr*) to end, turn.
Rows 3–5: 3 ch [counts as 1st dc (*UKtr*)], dc (*UKtr*) 2 tog to last st, 1 dc (*UKtr*) in last st. Fasten off.
Join silver metallic yarn to start of hat and work 1 row of sc (*UKdc*) all along the starting ch edge, fasten off.

Hat bobble
Using silver metallic yarn, make 3 ch. Work 12 dc (*UKtr*) into 3rd ch from hook, join with a sl st. Fasten off. Run thread through row of dc (*UKtr*) and draw up tightly into a little ball. Fasten off.

To make up
Work in all ends. Fold each foot in half and sew up the sides – the wide end is the front of the foot. Sew the feet to the base of the body, angling them outwards slightly. Sew a pupil to each eye then work a French knot in white in the centre of each eye. Place the eyes on the body, using the photograph as a guide, and sew in place. Fold the beak in half and sew the sides. Add a little stuffing to pad slightly. Sew the wide end of the beak to the head. Sew a wing to each side of the body. Sew the side seam of the hat and turn back a brim. Sew the bobble to the top. Pop a little stuffing in the hat then stitch it on to the penguin's head.

Cool Snowman

Materials and equipment:

Crochet hook size 2.00mm (US B-1, UK 14)

No. 3 crochet cotton – 1 ball of white and small amounts of black, green and orange

Scrap of mini tinsel

4 tiny black buttons

Tapestry needle, sewing needle and thread to match the yarns

Small amount of stuffing

Measurements:

The snowman is approximately 10cm (4in) tall.

Instructions:

Head

Using white crochet cotton, make 2 ch.
Round 1: work 6 sc (UKdc) into 2nd ch from hook then join with a sl st to form a tight circle.
Round 2: work 2 sc (UKdc) into each st around then join with a sl st.

Round 3: *1 sc (UKdc) into next sc (UKdc), 2 sc (UKdc) into next sc (UKdc),* repeat from * to * all around then join with a sl st as before.
Round 4: *1 sc (UKdc) into each of next 2 sc (UKdc), 2 sc (UKdc) into next sc (UKdc),* repeat from * to * all around then join with a sl st.
Rounds 5–9: work in sc (UKdc) all around.
You will now begin decreasing. Stuff the head before you close it up.
Round 10: *1 sc (UKdc) into each of next 2 sc (UKdc), sc (UKdc) 2 tog,* repeat from * to * all around then join with a sl st as before.
Round 11: work in sc (UKdc) all around.
Round 12: *1 sc (UKdc) into next sc (UKdc), sc (UKdc) 2 tog,* repeat from * to * all around then join with a sl st.
Round 13: work in sc (UKdc) all around.
Round 14: sc (UKdc) 2 tog all around then join with a sl st. Fasten off.

Body

Using white crochet cotton, make 2 ch.
Round 1: work 6 sc (UKdc) into 2nd ch from hook then join with a sl st to form a tight circle.
Round 2: 2 sc (UKdc) into each st around then join with a sl st [12 sts].
Round 3: *1 sc (UKdc) into next sc (UKdc), 2 sc (UKdc) into next sc (UKdc),* repeat from * to * all around then join with a sl st.
Round 4: *1 sc (UKdc) into each of next 2 sc (UKdc), 2 sc (UKdc) into next sc (UKdc),* repeat from * to * all around then join with a sl st.
Round 5: *1 sc (UKdc) into each of next 3 sc (UKdc), 2 sc (UKdc) into next sc (UKdc),* repeat from * to * all around then join with a sl st.
Rounds 6–20 work in sc (UKdc) all around. Fasten off.

Base

Using white crochet cotton, make 2 ch.
Round 1: work 6 sc (UKdc) into 2nd ch from hook then join with a sl st to form a tight circle.
Round 2: 2 sc (UKdc) into each st around then join with a sl st.
Round 3: *1 sc (UKdc) into next sc (UKdc), 2 sc (UKdc) into next sc (UKdc),* repeat from * to * all around then join with a sl st.

Round 4: *1 sc (UKdc) into each of next 2 sc (UKdc), 2 sc (UKdc) into next sc (UKdc),* repeat from * to * all around then join with a sl st. Work 1 round in sc (UKdc). Fasten off.

Hat

Using black crochet cotton, make 2 ch.
Round 1: work 6 sc (UKdc) into 2nd ch from hook then join with a sl st to form a tight circle.
Round 2: 2 sc (UKdc) into each st around then join with a sl st [12 sts].
Round 3: *1 sc (UKdc) into next sc (UKdc), 2 sc (UKdc) into next sc (UKdc),* repeat from * to * all around then join with a sl st [18 sts].
Rounds 4–5: work in sc (UKdc) all around.
Round 6: work 2 sc (UKdc) into each sc (UKdc) all around then join with a sl st.
Round 7: work in sc (UKdc) all around.
Fasten off.

Scarf

Using green crochet cotton, make 36 ch.
Row 1: work 1 sc (UKdc) into 2nd ch from hook, 1 sc (UKdc) into each ch to end.
Rows 2–3: work in sc (UKdc) to end. Fasten off.

To make up

Work in all the ends. Stuff the body lightly and then sew the base to the body. Invert the base slightly to make the snowman stand up. Sew the hat on to the head. Embroider the features with black and orange, using the photograph as a guide. Now attach the head to the body. Sew the buttons to the front of the snowman. Wrap mini tinsel around the hat and secure with a stitch. Wrap the scarf around the snowman's neck and secure with a few stitches. Make a hanging loop by crocheting a chain of black cotton, if required, and attach it to the top of the hat.

Little Angel

Materials and equipment:

Crochet hook size 2.00mm (US B-1, UK 14)

No. 3 crochet cotton – 1 ball of pale pink, 1 ball of white and a small amount of black for the features

Small amount of silver metallic yarn

Silver ribbon bow

0.5m (20in) narrow white ribbon

Small piece of gold cushion piping for the hair

Sewing needles and thread to match the yarns

Small amount of stuffing

Craft glue

Measurements:

The angel is approximately 9cm (3½in) tall.

Instructions:

Head

Using pale pink crochet cotton, make 2 ch.
Round 1: work 6 sc (*UKdc*) into 2nd ch from hook then join with a sl st to form a tight circle.
Round 2: work 2 sc (*UKdc*) into each st around [12 sts].
Round 3: *1 sc (*UKdc*) into next sc (*UKdc*), 2 sc (*UKdc*) into next sc (*UKdc*),* repeat from * to * all around [18 sts].
Round 4: *1 sc (*UKdc*) into each of next 2 sc (*UKdc*), 2 sc (*UKdc*) into next sc (*UKdc*),* repeat from * to * all around [24 sts].
Rounds 5–9: work in sc (*UKdc*) all around.
You will now begin decreasing. Stuff the head before you close it up.
Round 10: *1 sc (*UKdc*) into each of next 2 sc (*UKdc*), sc (*UKdc*) 2 tog,* repeat from * to * all around.
Round 11: work in sc (*UKdc*) all around.
Round 12: *1 sc (*UKdc*) into next sc (*UKdc*), sc (*UKdc*) 2 tog,* repeat from * to * all around.
Round 13: work in sc (*UKdc*) all around.
Round 14: sc (*UKdc*) 2 tog all around then join with a sl st. Fasten off.

Body

Using white crochet cotton, make 2 sc (*UKdc*).
Round 1: work 6 sc (*UKdc*) into 2nd ch from hook then join with a sl st to form a tight circle.
Round 2: 2 sc (*UKdc*) into each st around [12 sts].
Round 3: *1 sc (*UKdc*) into next sc (*UKdc*), 2 sc (*UKdc*) into next sc (*UKdc*),* repeat from * to * all around [18 sts].
Round 4: *1 sc (*UKdc*) into each of next 2 sc (*UKdc*), 2 sc (*UKdc*) into next sc (*UKdc*),* repeat from * to * all around [24 sts].
Round 5: *1 sc (*UKdc*) into each of next 3 sc (*UKdc*), 2 sc (*UKdc*) into next sc (*UKdc*),* repeat from * to * all around [30 sts].
Rounds 6–14: work in sc (*UKdc*) all around.
Fasten off.

Base

Using white crochet cotton, work as body up to end of round 3.

Dress (worked from neck down)

Using white crochet cotton, make 10 ch then join with a sl st into a ring.
Round 1: into the ring work 2 ch, 15 sc (*UKdc*) then join with a sl st [16 sc (*UKdc*)].

Round 2: 2 ch, 1 dc (UKtr) into same st, 2 dc (UKtr) into each sc (UKdc) to end, join with a sl st [32 dc (UKtr)].
Round 3: 2 ch, 1 dc (UKtr) in same st, 2 dc (UKtr) into each of next 5 dc (UKtr), 4 ch, miss next 4 ch, 2 dc (UKtr) into each of next 12 dc (UKtr), 4 ch, miss next 4 ch, 2 dc (UKtr) into remaining 6 dc (UKtr), join with a sl st.
Round 4: *3 ch, miss 1 dc (UKtr), sc (UKdc) into next dc (UKtr) or st,* repeat from * to * all around, do not join.
Round 5: *3 ch, 1 sc (UKdc) into 3 ch loop of previous round,* repeat from * to * all around.
Round 6: join in silver yarn and work as previous row.
Repeat last 2 rows once more. Break silver and continue in white until you have eight 3 ch loop rows in all. Break white and join in silver.
Next round: *3 dc (UKtr), 3 ch, 3 dc (UKtr) into next 3 ch loop, 1 sc (UKdc) into next 3 ch loop,* repeat from * to * all around, ending with 3 dc (UKtr), 3 ch, 3 dc (UKtr), sl st to beg of round. Fasten off.

Arms (make 2)
Using pale pink crochet cotton, make 13 ch.
Row 1: 1 sc (UKdc) into 2nd ch from hook, 1 sc (UKdc) into each ch to end, turn.
Rows 2–4: 1 ch, 1 sc (UKdc) into each sc (UKdc) to end, turn. Fasten off.

Halo
Using silver yarn, make 2 ch.
Round 1: work 6 sc (UKdc) into 2nd ch from hook then join with sl st into a circle.
Round 2: 1 ch, work 2 sc (UKdc) into each sc (UKdc) around then join with sl st as before.
Round 3: *3 ch, 1 sc (UKdc) into next sc (UKdc),* repeat from * to * all around, join as before. Fasten off.

Wings (make 2)
Using white crochet cotton, make 2 ch.
Row 1: work 6 dc (UKtr) into 2nd ch from hook, turn.
Row 2: 3 ch, 1 dc (UKtr) into first st, 2 dc (UKtr) into each st to end, turn.
Row 3: repeat row 2.
Row 4: join in silver yarn and work 1 sc (UKdc) into each st to end, turn.
Row 5: work 2 sc (UKdc) into each sc (UKdc) to end. Fasten off.

To make up
Sew in any loose ends on all pieces. Stuff the body and attach the base. Invert the base a little to enable the angel to stand up. Place the body inside the dress, thread ribbon through the waist of the dress and tie it firmly to hold the body inside, adding a few stitches if needed; trim the ends. Sew the silver ribbon bow on to the front of the dress.

Fold each arm in half lengthways and stitch the sides. Position an arm on each side of the angel, pushing it through the armhole of the dress. Sew these in place. Sew the other ends of the arms together, pinching them a little in prayer. Secure with a few stitches. Sew the wings together in the centre then stitch them in place on the back of the angel.

Unwind the strands of the gold cushion piping using a needle to tease the strands out into ringlets. Cut the strands into equal lengths and glue them to the top of the angel's head; trim them to a nice shape. Sew the halo to the back of the head. Embroider the features using black. Finally, attach the head to the body.

Christmas Cracker

Materials and equipment:

Crochet hook size 2.00mm (US B-1, UK 14)

No. 5 crochet cotton – 1 ball of green and 1 ball of red

1m (40in) of narrow red satin ribbon

0.5m (20in) of gold ric-rac braid

1 gold rose embellishment

Small piece of card

Small amount of stuffing

Sewing needle and thread to match the yarns

Measurements:

The cracker is approximately 14cm (5½in) long.

Instructions:

Using green crochet cotton, make 27 ch.
Row 1: work 1 dc (*UKtr*) into 3rd ch from hook, 1 dc (*UKtr*) into each ch to end, turn.
Row 2: 1 ch, work 1 sc (*UKdc*) into each dc (*UKtr*) to end, turn.
Row 3: 3 ch, miss first st, work 1 dc (*UKtr*) into each sc (*UKdc*) to end, turn.
Row 4: repeat row 2.

Change to red cotton.
Rows 5–14: repeat rows 3 and 4 five times.

Change to green cotton.
Rows 15–18: repeat rows 3 and 4 twice.
Fasten off.

To make up

Work in the ends. Fold the crochet lengthways to form a tube and then sew the long edges together, matching the colours and rows. The seam will be on the underside of the piece.

Measure a piece of card slightly shorter than the inner red section of the cracker. Roll it into a tube then try the tube inside the crochet to get a good fit. When you are happy with the size, glue the edges of the card together and slip the tube inside the cracker.

Add some stuffing to the inside of the tube to give the cracker more body. Cut the red ribbon into two lengths and tie one tightly to each end of the cracker either side of the tube section, using the photograph as a guide. Trim the ribbon if necessary for a smart finish. Measure a piece of gold ric-rac braid long enough to fit around the central red section and glue it in place with the join on the underside. Glue the gold rose embellishment to the centre as shown in the photograph.

Tip

Hide the join on the ric-rac braid under the rose embellishment for a super-neat finish.

Wishing Star

Materials and equipment:

Crochet hook size 2.00mm (US B-1, UK 14)

No. 5 crochet cotton – 1 ball of white (this is sufficient to make several stars)

Small amount of metallic silver yarn

0.5m (20in) of narrow white ribbon

1 large sparkly button

Sewing needle and white thread

Measurements:

The star is approximately 8cm (3¼in) in diameter.

Instructions:

Using white crochet cotton, make 6 ch then join with a sl st into a ring.

Round 1: 1 ch, work 12 sc (UKdc) into the ring then join with sl st to first ch.

Round 2: 5 ch, miss 1 sc (UKdc), sc (UKdc) into next sc (UKdc), all around, join to 1st of 5 ch at beg of round [six 5 ch loops].

Round 3: sl st into first 5 ch loop, 2 ch, work 5 dc (UKtr) into same loop, 1 sc (UKdc) in next sc (UKdc). *6 dc (UKtr) into 5 ch loop, 1 sc (UKdc) into next sc (UKdc),* repeat from * to * 4 times more and then join with a sl st to beg of round.

Round 4: sl st to 2nd dc (UKtr), 2 ch, 1 dc (UKtr) into same dc (UKtr), 2 dc (UKtr) into each of next 3 dc (UKtr), 1 sc (UKdc) into next sc (UKdc), *miss next dc (UKtr), 2 dc (UKtr) into each of next 4 dc (UKtr), miss 1 dc (UKtr), 1 sc (UKdc) into sc (UKdc),* repeat from * to * 4 times more and then join with a sl st to beg of round. Break off white.

Round 5: join in metallic yarn to same place as sl st and proceed as follows. Work *1 sc (UKdc) into each of the next 4 dc (UKtr), **4 ch, sl st into 3rd ch from hook (1 picot formed),** repeat from ** to ** twice more, 1 sc (UKdc) into each of the next 4 dc (UKtr), 1 sc (UKdc) into sc (UKdc) of row 4, thus pulling up a long loop,* repeat from * to * 5 times more and then join with a sl st to beg of round. Fasten off.

To make up

Using white thread, stitch the large sparkly button to the centre front of the star. Thread the ribbon through the top of one point to make a hanging loop. Decide how long you want the ribbon loop to be and trim the ribbon as necessary. Either tie the ends of the ribbon together in a knot or stitch them to form a loop.

Christmas Bell

Materials and equipment:

Crochet hook size 2.00mm (US B-1, UK 14)

No. 5 crochet cotton – 1 ball of white

2 burgundy organza ribbon embellishments

0.5m (20in) gold-edged burgundy ribbon

Spray fabric stiffener

Craft glue

Measurements:

The bell is approximately 6cm (2¼in) high, excluding the ribbon.

Instructions:

Using white crochet cotton, make 8 ch then join with a sl st into a ring.

Round 1: work 16 sc (UKdc) into the ring then join with a sl st.

Round 2: 6 ch, *miss 1 sc (UKdc), 1 dc (UKtr) into next sc (UKdc), 2 ch,* repeat all around, join to 3rd ch of 6 ch at beg of round.

Round 3: sl st to first 2 ch sp, 3 ch, 2 dc (UKtr), 1 ch, 3 dc (UKtr) into same space, *1 sc (UKdc) into next sp, 3 dc (UKtr), 1 ch, 3 dc (UKtr) into next sp,* repeat from * to * twice more, 1 sc (UKdc) into last sp, join to base of first dc (UKtr) of round with a sl st.

Round 4: 5 ch, *4 dc (UKtr), 2 ch, 4 dc (UKtr) into centre of next group, 1 dc (UKtr) into next sc (UKdc),* repeat from * to *, ending last repeat with 1 sl st into 3rd ch of 5 ch at the start of the round.

Round 5: 5 ch, *5 dc (UKtr), 3 ch, 5 dc (UKtr) into centre of next group, 1 dc (UKtr) into next dc (UKtr),* repeat from * to * ending last repeat with 1 sl st into 3rd ch of 5 ch at start of round.

Round 6: 8 ch, 1 sc (UKdc) into centre of next group, *5 ch, 1 dc (UKtr) into next dc (UKtr), 5 ch, 1 sc (UKdc) into centre of next group,* repeat from * to * ending with sl st into 3rd ch of 8 ch made at beg of round.

Round 7: *into next 5 ch sp work [1 sc (UKdc), 1 hdc (UKhtr), 1 dc (UKtr), 1 hdc (UKhtr), 1 sc (UKdc)], 1 sc (UKdc) in next sc (UKdc) or dc (UKtr),* repeat from * to * all around, join with a sl st.

Round 8: * work 1 sc (UKdc) into each sc (UKdc) to dc (UKtr) at point of each group, 3 ch, sl st into base of st just worked (picot made), * repeat from * to * all around, join with a sl st. Fasten off.

Bell clapper

Using white crochet cotton, make 3 ch, work 10 dc (UKtr) into 2nd ch from hook, join with a sl st. Fasten off then run thread through last row, draw up tight into a ball and fasten off. Crochet a chain 5cm (2in) long then fasten off. Attach the ball to the end of the chain firmly.

To make up

Work in all yarn ends on the bell. Spray the bell with starch and then stretch it to shape over a suitable container. Leave it to dry. Pull out the picot points as the starch dries to give a nice shape. When the bell is dry, attach the clapper inside by threading the chain through the hole at the top of the bell and gluing it in place. Make a loop of ribbon and thread it through the top hole in the bell; glue the ends in place. Attach the two organza flowers on either side.

Snowy Fridge Magnet

Materials and equipment:

Crochet hook size 2.00mm (US B-1, UK 14)

No. 5 crochet cotton – 1 ball of white, 1 ball of mid blue and small amounts of black, red, and orange

Silver metallic yarn for the edging

A few small white beads

Small wooden Christmas-tree embellishment, approximately 4cm (1½in) high

Craft glue

Magnetic photo paper

Embroidery needle

Measurements:

The fridge magnet is approximately 8cm (3½in) square.

Instructions:

Background

Using white crochet cotton, make 20 ch.
Row 1: work 1 sc (*UKdc*) into 2nd ch from hook, 1 sc (*UKdc*) into each ch to end, turn.
Row 2: 1 ch, work 1 sc (*UKdc*) into each ch to end, turn.
Rows 3–8: repeat row 2.
Change to mid blue and work 14 rows in sc (*UKdc*). Fasten off.
Join mid blue to any corner of the background crochet. Work 1 round of sc (*UKdc*) all around the piece, working into row ends or stitches; work 3 sc (*UKdc*) into each corner to keep the work flat. Break mid blue and join in silver to work a further round of sc (*UKdc*), treating the corners as before; join to beg with a sl st. Fasten off.

Snowman's head

Using white crochet cotton, make 6 ch then join with a sl st to form a tight ring.
Round 1: work 1 sc (*UKdc*) into each ch to end and then join with a sl st.
Round 2: 1 ch, work 2 sc (*UKdc*) into each sc (*UKdc*) to end and then join as before. Fasten off.

Snowman's body

Using white crochet cotton, make 6 ch then join with a sl st to form a tight ring.
Round 1: work 1 sc (*UKdc*) into each ch to end, join with a sl st.
Round 2: 1 ch, work 2 sc (*UKdc*) into each sc (*UKdc*) to end, join as before.
Round 3: 1 ch, work *1 sc (*UKdc*) into next sc (*UKdc*), 2 sc (*UKdc*) into next sc (*UKdc*),* repeat from * to * all around, join with a sl st.
Round 4: 1 ch, work *1 sc (*UKdc*) into each of next 2 sc (*UKdc*), 2 sc (*UKdc*) into next sc (*UKdc*),* repeat from * to * all around, join with a sl st. Fasten off.

Snowman's scarf

Using red crochet cotton, make 30 ch and then fasten off.

Snowman's hat

Using black crochet cotton, make 7 ch.
Row 1: 1 ch, work 1 sc (*UKdc*) into each ch to end, turn.
Row 2: *sl st over 2 sc (*UKdc*),* repeat from * to * to last 2 sc (*UKdc*), turn.
Rows 3–4: work each st in sc (*UKdc*). Fasten off.

To make up

Cut a piece of magnetic photo paper the same size as the crocheted background. Using craft glue, stick the paper on to the back of the crocheted background. Press down firmly and allow it to adhere. Sew the snowman's head to his body with a few stitches. Wrap the scarf around his neck and secure. Embroider tiny black dots for eyes and an orange nose. Glue the hat in place on the snowman's head. Stick the snowman on to one side of the background and the tree on to the other, using the photograph as a guide. Glue tiny white beads on to the blue area of the background to suggest falling snow.

Christmas Pudding

Materials and equipment:

Crochet hook size 2.00mm (US B-1, UK 14)

Metallic yarn – 1 ball of brown

No. 3 crochet cotton – small amount of white

0.5m (20in) of white ribbon

Holly berry embellishment

Small amount of stuffing

Craft glue

Measurements:

The Christmas pudding is approximately 6cm (2¼in) high.

Instructions:

Using brown metallic yarn, make 2 ch, work 6 sc (UKdc) into 2nd ch from hook then join with a sl st into a ring.

Round 1: work 2 sc (UKdc) into each sc (UKdc) around, join with a sl st.

Round 2: *1 sc (UKdc) into next sc (UKdc), 2 sc (UKdc) into next sc (UKdc),* repeat from * to * all around and then join into a circle with a sl st as before.

Round 3: *1 sc (UKdc) into each of next 2 sc (UKdc), 2 sc (UKdc) into next sc (UKdc),* repeat from * to * all around and then join with sl st as before.

Round 4: *1 sc (UKdc) into each of next 3 sc (UKdc), 2 sc (UKdc) into next sc (UKdc),* repeat from * to * all around and then join with a sl st as before.

Round 5: 1 sc (UKdc) into each of next 4 sc (UKdc), 2 sc (UKdc) into next sc (UKdc),* repeat from * to * all around and then join with sl st as before.

Work 8 rounds in sc (UKdc) with no increase. Now you will start the decreases. Stuff the pudding as you go.

Next round: *1 sc (UKdc) into each of next 4 sc (UKdc), sc (UKdc) 2 tog,* repeat from * to * all around and then join with a sl st as before.

Next round: *1 sc (UKdc) into each of next 3 sc (UKdc), sc (UKdc) 2 tog,* repeat from * to * all around and then join with a sl st as before.

Next round: *1 sc (UKdc) into each of next 2 sc (UKdc), sc (UKdc) 2 tog,* repeat from * to * all around and then join with a sl st as before.

Next round: *1 sc (UKdc) into next sc (UKdc), sc (UKdc) 2 tog,* repeat from * to * all around and then join as before.

Next round: sc (UKdc) 2 tog all around. Cut the yarn, run the end through the last row of sts, draw up and fasten off.

Iced topping

Using white crochet cotton, make 2 ch. Work 6 sc (UKdc) into 2nd ch from hook then join with a sl st into a ring.

Round 1: (RS) work 2 sc (UKdc) into each sc (UKdc) all around and then join with a sl st.

Round 2: *1 sc (UKdc) into next sc (UKdc), 2 sc (UKdc) into next sc (UKdc),* repeat from * to * all around and then join with a sl st as before.

Round 3: *1 sc (UKdc) into each of next 2 sc (UKdc), 2 sc (UKdc) into next sc (UKdc),* repeat from * to * all around and then join with a sl st as before.

Round 4: *1 sc (*UKdc*) into each of next 3 sc (*UKdc*), 2 sc (*UKdc*) into next sc (*UKdc*),* repeat from * to * all around and then join with a sl st as before.

Round 5: 1 sc (*UKdc*) into each of next 4 sc (*UKdc*), 2 sc (*UKdc*) into next sc (*UKdc*),* repeat from * to * all around and then join with a sl st as before.

Work 4 rounds in sc (*UKdc*) without further shaping.

Next round: working with the WS facing: *1 dc (*UKtr*) into next sc (*UKdc*), sl st into next sc (*UKdc*),* repeat from * to * all around and then join as before. Fasten off.

To make up

Work in any loose ends neatly. Place the iced topping over one end of the pudding and stitch in place all around. Push the holly embellishment through the centre of the icing and secure it with a few stitches or a little craft glue.

Thread the ribbon through the top of the pudding to make a hanging loop. Decide how long you want the ribbon loop to be and trim the ribbon as necessary. Either tie the ends of the ribbon together in a knot or stitch them to form a loop.

Tabletop Tree

Materials and equipment:

Crochet hook size 2.00mm (US B-1, UK 14)

No. 3 crochet cotton – 1 ball of green and 1 ball of variegated green

Scrap of mini tinsel

Mini coloured tinsel balls

2 gold stars

Cocktail stick

Craft glue

Small amount of stuffing

Measurements:

The tree is approximately 8cm (3¼in) high.

Instructions:

Tree

Using green crochet cotton, make 40 ch and join with a sl st into a circle, being careful not to twist the chain.

Round 1: work 1 sc (UKdc) into each ch around then join with a sl st to beg of round [40 sts].

Work a further 3 rounds of sc (UKdc).

Round 5: *1 sc (UKdc) into each of next 3 sc (UKdc), sc (UKdc) 2 tog,* repeat from * to * all around [32 sts].

Work 4 rounds in sc (UKdc).

Next round: *1 sc (UKdc) into each of next 2 sc (UKdc), sc (UKdc) 2 tog,* repeat from * to * all around [24 sts].

Work 4 rounds in sc (UKdc).

Next round: *1 sc (UKdc) into next sc (UKdc), sc (UKdc) 2 tog,* repeat from * to * all around [16 sts].

Work 4 rounds in sc (UKdc).

Next round: sc (UKdc) 2 tog all around [8 sts].

Work 2 rounds in sc (UKdc).

Next round: sc (UKdc) 2 tog all around.

Fasten off.

Base

Using green, make 2 ch.

Round 1: work 6 sc (UKdc) into 2nd ch from hook then join with a sl st into a tight circle.

Round 2: 2 sc (UKdc) into each st around then join with a sl st to beg [12 sts].

Round 3: *1 sc (UKdc) into next sc (UKdc), 2 sc (UKdc) into next sc (UKdc),* repeat from * to * all around then join with a sl st as before [18 sts].

Round 4: *1 sc (UKdc) into each of next 2 sc (UKdc), 2 sc (UKdc) into next sc (UKdc),* repeat from * to * all around then join with a sl st [24 sts].

Round 5: * 1 sc (UKdc) into each of next 3 sc (UKdc), 2 sc (UKdc) into next sc (UKdc),* repeat from * to * all around then join with a sl st [30 sts].

Round 6: 1 sc (UKdc) into each of next 4 sc (UKdc), 2 sc (UKdc) into next sc (UKdc),* repeat from * to * all around then join with a sl st [36 sts].

Round 7: 1 sc (UKdc) into each of next 5 sc (UKdc), 2 sc (UKdc) into next sc (UKdc),* repeat from * to * all around then join with a sl st [42 sts]. Fasten off.

Twisted strands (make 1 in each of 4 sizes)

Using variegated green crochet cotton, make 20 ch. Work 1 dc (*UKtr*) into 3rd ch from hook, then 3 dc (*UKtr*) into each ch to end. The crochet will twist as you work. Fasten off. Repeat the process starting with 28 ch, 30 ch and 36 ch.

To make up

Work in all the ends. Stuff the tree quite firmly then attach the base, inverting it slightly to enable the tree to stand. Take each twisted strand and sew the ends together to form a circle. Place the circles on the tree in size order, starting with the largest at the base. Sew in place. Wrap some tinsel around the tree, securing it with a little craft glue or stitches. Glue the tinsel balls on to the branches at random. Cut the cocktail stick in half. Place a little glue on one side of a star and press the other star on to it, sandwiching half the cocktail stick in between. Press firmly until well stuck. Push the cocktail stick down into the top of the tree, securing it with a little glue.

Yuletide Coaster

Materials and equipment:

Crochet hook size 2.00mm (US B-1, UK 14)

No. 3 crochet cotton – 1 ball of bright red and small amounts of dark red, variegated green and dark green

Small amount of metallic yarn in dark green

Sewing needle and thread to match the yarns

Measurements:

The coaster is approximately 13cm (5in) square.

Instructions:

Using bright red, make 27 ch.

Row 1: (RS) work 1 sc (UKdc) into 2nd ch from hook, 1 sc (UKdc) into each ch to end, turn [26 sts].

Row 2: 1 ch, *1 sc (UKdc) into next sc (UKdc), 1 dc (UKtr) into next sc (UKdc),* repeat from * to * to end, turn.

Row 3: 1 ch, miss 1 st, *1 dc (UKtr) into next sc (UKdc), 1 sc (UKdc) into next dc (UKtr),* repeat from * to * to last st, 1 dc (UKtr) into last st, turn. Rows 2 and 3 form the pattern and are repeated. Work a further 4 rows in pattern.

Join in variegated green yarn, and work 2 rows in pattern.

Break green and continue in bright red, working the 2 pattern rows until the piece measures 13cm (5in). Fasten off.

Edging

Join the variegated green yarn to any corner and work 1 round of sc (UKdc) all around, working 3 sc (UKdc) into each corner to keep the work flat.

Next row: turn the work so that the WS is facing and work *1 dc (UKtr) into next sc (UKdc), sl st into next sc (UKdc),* repeat from * to * all around then fasten off.

Holly leaf

Using metallic green, make 8 ch, 1 sc (UKdc) into 2nd ch from hook, *1 hdc (UKhtr) in next ch, 3 ch, 1 sl st into top of hdc (UKhtr), 1 sc (UKdc) into next ch,* repeat from * to * twice more. Now work in the same way along the other side of the starting ch; sl st into last ch and then fasten off.

Repeat to make a second leaf using dark green.

Berry

Using dark red, make 3 ch, work 12 dc (UKtr) into 2nd ch from hook then join with a sl st. Break the yarn and run through top of sts; draw up into a tight ball.

To make up

Work in the ends on all pieces. Press the coaster lightly using a damp cloth and warm iron to flatten it. Arrange the holly leaves and berry on the coaster using the photograph as a guide. Sew them in place.

Festive Napkin Ring

Materials and equipment:

Crochet hook size 2.00mm (US B-1, UK 14)

No. 5 crochet cotton – 1 ball of white

Gold metallic yarn

Needle and white thread

Measurements:

The napkin ring is approximately 8cm (3¼in) wide and 6cm (2¼in) tall and will fit an average napkin.

Instructions:

Napkin ring

Using white crochet cotton, make 16 ch.

Row 1: work 1 sc (*UKdc*) into 2nd ch from hook, 1 sc (*UKdc*) into each ch to end, turn.

Rows 2–7 form the pattern. Carry the gold yarn neatly up the side of the work as you proceed, twisting the yarns together to keep them neat.

Rows 2–5: using white, 1 ch, work 1 sc (*UKdc*) into each sc (*UKdc*) to end, turn.

Rows 6–7: using gold metallic yarn, repeat row 2.

Work 8 more pattern repeats, then work rows 2–5 one more time. Fasten off.

Join white yarn to one long edge, with the WS facing. Work *1 dc (*UKtr*), 1 sc (*UKdc*),* repeat from * to * all along the edge, fasten off. Repeat along the other long edge.

Rose petals

Using white crochet cotton, make 6 ch then join with a sl st into a ring.

Round 1: 1 ch, work 12 sc (*UKdc*) into the ring, join with a sl st to first ch.

Round 2: *5 ch, miss 1 sc (*UKdc*), 1 sc (*UKdc*) into next sc (*UKdc*),* repeat from * to * all around, join to 1st of 5 ch at beg of round [six 5 ch loops].

Round 3: sl st into first 5 ch loop, 2 ch, work 5 dc (*UKtr*) into same loop, 1 sc (*UKdc*) in next sc (*UKdc*), *6 dc (*UKtr*) into 5 ch loop, 1 sc (*UKdc*) into next sc (*UKdc*),* repeat from * to * 4 times more and then join with a sl st to beg of round.

Round 4: sl st to 2nd dc (*UKtr*), 2 ch, 1 dc (*UKtr*) into same dc (*UKtr*), 2 dc (*UKtr*) into each of next 3 dc (*UKtr*), 1 sc (*UKdc*) into next sc (*UKdc*), *miss next dc (*UKtr*), 2 dc (*UKtr*) into each of next 4 dc (*UKtr*), miss 1 dc (*UKtr*), 1 sc (*UKdc*) into sc (*UKdc*),* repeat from * to * 4 times more and then join with a sl st to beg of round. Break off yarn.

Round 5: join in gold to same place as sl st and work *1 sc (*UKdc*) into each of the next 4 dc (*UKtr*), 3 ch, sl st into 1st of the these ch (1 picot formed), 1 sc (*UKdc*) into each of the next 4 dc (*UKtr*), 1 sc (*UKdc*) into corresponding sc (*UKdc*) of row 3, thus pulling up a long loop,* repeat from * to * 5 times more, join with a sl st to beg of round. Fasten off.

Rose centre

Using white crochet cotton, make 30 ch.

Row 1: work 1 dc (*UKtr*) into 3rd ch from hook, 3 dc (*UKtr*) into each ch to end.

Break white and join in gold, turn.

Row 2: work 1 sc (*UKdc*) into each dc (*UKtr*) to end.

To make up

Join the shorts ends of the napkin ring neatly and work in all the yarn ends. Work in all ends on the rose pieces. Coil the rose centre tightly and sew in place on the petals. Sew the flower to the napkin ring.

Christmas Bear

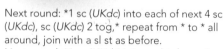

Materials and equipment:

Crochet hook sizes 2.00mm (US B-1, UK 14) and
  4.00mm (US G-6, UK 8)

No. 3 crochet cotton – 1 ball of beige,
  1 ball of red and small amounts
  of mid brown, dark brown and green

Small amount of white eyelash yarn

1 tiny red bead

Gold jingle bell

0.5m (20in) of narrow red ribbon

Sewing needle and thread to match
  the yarns

Small amount of stuffing

Measurements:

The bear measures approximately
14cm (5½in) from the end of his hat
to the tip of his nose

Instructions:

Head

Using the 2.00mm (US B-1, UK 14) hook and
beige yarn, make 2 ch. Work 6 sc (UKdc) into
2nd ch from hook then join with a sl st into
a circle.
Round 1: work 2 sc (UKdc) into each sc (UKdc)
around then join with a sl st [12 sts].
Round 2: *1 sc (UKdc) into next sc (UKdc), 2 sc
(UKdc) into next sc (UKdc),* repeat from * to *
all around, join with a sl st as before.
Round 3: *1 sc (UKdc) into each of next 2 sc
(UKdc), 2 sc (UKdc) into next sc (UKdc),* repeat
from * to * all around, join with a sl st as before.
Round 4: *1 sc (UKdc) into each of next 3 sc
(UKdc), 2 sc (UKdc) into next sc (UKdc),* repeat
from * to * all around, join with a sl st as before.
Round 5: 1 sc (UKdc) into each of next 4 sc
(UKdc), 2 sc (UKdc) into next sc (UKdc),* repeat
from * to * all around, join with a sl st as before.
Work 8 rounds in sc (UKdc) with no increase.
Now shape the top, stuffing the head as
you go.

Next round: *1 sc (UKdc) into each of next 4 sc
(UKdc), sc (UKdc) 2 tog,* repeat from * to * all
around, join with a sl st as before.
Next round: *1 sc (UKdc) into each of next 3 sc
(UKdc), sc (UKdc) 2 tog,* repeat from * to * all
around, join with a sl st as before.
Next round: *1 sc (UKdc) into each of next 2 sc
(UKdc), sc (UKdc) 2 tog,* repeat from * to * all
around, join with a sl st as before.
Next round: *1 sc (UKdc) into next sc (UKdc), sc
(UKdc) 2 tog,* repeat from * to * all around, join
with a sl st as before.
Next round: sc (UKdc) 2 tog all around. Fasten
off and run thread through last row of sts; draw
up and fasten off.

Muzzle

Using the 2.00mm (US B-1, UK 14) hook and
mid brown yarn, make 2 ch. Work 6 sc (UKdc)
into 2nd ch from hook then join with a sl st into
a circle.
Round 1: work 2 sc (UKdc) into each sc (UKdc)
to end, join with a sl st [12 sts].

Round 2: *1 sc (UKdc) into next sc (UKdc), 2 sc (UKdc) into next sc (UKdc),* repeat from * to * all around, join with a sl st as before.
Round 3: *1 sc (UKdc) into next 2 sc (UKdc), 2 sc (UKdc) into next sc (UKdc),* repeat from * to * all around, join with a sl st as before. Fasten off.

Ear (make 1)
Using the 2.00mm (US B-1, UK 14) hook and mid brown yarn make 2 ch. Work 6 sc (UKdc) into 2nd ch from hook then join with a sl st into a circle.
Round 1: work 2 sc (UKdc) into each sc (UKdc) to end, join with a sl st.
Round 2: work 1 sc (UKdc) into each sc (UKdc) to end. Fasten off.

Hat
Using the 2.00mm (US B-1, UK 14) hook and red yarn make 32 ch.
Row 1: 1 hdc (UKhtr) into 3rd ch from hook, 1 hdc (UKhtr) into each ch to end, turn.
Row 2: 1 ch, 1 sc (UKdc) into each hdc (UKhtr) to end, turn.
Row 3: 2 ch [counts as first hdc (UKhtr)], 1 hdc (UKhtr) into each sc (UKdc) to end.
Row 4: repeat row 2.
Row 5: 2 ch [counts as first hdc (UKhtr)], 1 hdc (UKhtr) into each of next 2 hdc (UKhtr) ,* hdc (UKhtr) 2 tog, 1 hdc (UKhtr) into each of next 3 hdc (UKhtr),* repeat from * to * ending last repeat with hdc (UKhtr) 2 tog, hdc (UKhtr) into each of last 2 sc (UKdc). Turn.
Row 6: 1 ch, 1 sc (UKdc) into each sc (UKdc) to end.
Row 7: 2 ch [counts as first hdc (UKhtr)], *hdc (UKhtr) 2 tog, 1 hdc (UKhtr) into next sc (UKdc),* repeat from * to * ending last repeat with hdc (UKhtr) 2 tog, hdc (UKhtr) into each of last 2 sc (UKdc). Turn.
Row 8: repeat row 6.
Row 9: 2 ch [counts as first hdc (UKhtr)], *hdc (UKhtr) 2 tog,* repeat from * to * to last st, hdc (UKhtr) into last sc (UKdc).
Rows 10–15: work in hdc (UKhtr).
Row 16: hdc (UKhtr) 2 tog to end of row. Fasten off.
Using the 4.00mm (US G-6, UK 8) hook and eyelash yarn, make a chain long enough to wrap around the brim of the hat twice, fasten off.

Holly leaf (make 2)
Using the 2.00mm (US B-1, UK 14) hook and green yarn, make 5 ch. 1 sc (UKdc) into 2nd ch from hook, 2 ch, *sl st into top of sc (UKdc) just worked, 1 sc (UKdc) into next ch, 2 ch, sl st into top of sc (UKdc) just worked,* repeat from * to * once more. Fasten off.
Sew the leaves together as a pair. Sew a tiny red bead on to one end of the leaf to depict a berry.

To make up
Sew in any loose ends. Sew the hat seam and attach the bell to the point at the top. Wrap the eyelash chain twice around the brim of the hat to make a fluffy border and stitch it in place. Attach the holly leaf to one side of the hat.

Sew the muzzle on to the front of the head, stuffing it lightly to give it shape. Using dark brown, embroider the nose, mouth, eyes and eyebrows. Sew the ear in position. Only one ear is used because the hat sits on the other side of the head. Sew the hat to the head.

Thread the ribbon through the hat to make a hanging loop. Decide how long you want the ribbon loop to be and trim the ribbon as necessary. Either tie the ends of the ribbon together in a knot or stitch them to form a loop.

Poinsettia Gift Topper

Materials and equipment:

Crochet hook size 2.00mm (US B-1, UK 14)

Metallic yarn – 1 ball each of red, green and gold

90cm (35½in) of red gold-edged satin ribbon, 2.5cm (1in) wide

Gold flower bead stamens

Fine florist's wire or rose wire

Sewing needle and red thread

Measurements:

Each flower is approximately 6cm (2¼in) in diameter.

Instructions:

Flower 1 (6 petals)

Using red yarn, make 6 ch then join with sl st into a ring.

Round 1: 1 ch, work 12 sc (UKdc) into the ring, join with a sl st to first ch.

Round 2: *5 ch, miss 1 sc (UKdc), 1 sc (UKdc) into next sc (UKdc),* repeat from * to * all around, join to 1st of 5 ch at beg of round [six 5 ch loops].

Round 3: sl st into first 5 ch loop, 2 ch, work 5 dc (UKtr) into same loop, 1 sc (UKdc) in next sc (UKdc), *6 dc (UKtr) into 5 ch loop, 1 sc (UKdc) into next sc (UKdc),* repeat from * to * 4 times more, join with a sl st to beg of round.

Round 4: sl st to 2nd dc (UKtr), 2 ch, 1 dc (UKtr) into same dc (UKtr), 2 dc (UKtr) into each of next 3 dc (UKtr), 1 sc (UKdc) into next sc (UKdc),* miss next dc (UKtr), 2 dc (UKtr) into each of next 4 dc (UKtr), miss 1 dc (UKtr), 1 sc (UKdc) into sc (UKdc),* repeat from * to * 4 times more and then join with a sl st to beg of round. Break off red.

Round 5: join in gold to same place as sl st and work *1 sc (UKdc) into each of the next 4 dc (UKtr), 3 ch, sl st into 1st of the these ch (1 picot formed), 1 sc (UKdc) into each of the next 4 dc (UKtr), 1 sc (UKdc) into corresponding sc (UKdc) of row 3, thus pulling up a long loop,* repeat from * to * 5 times more, join with a sl st to beg of round. Fasten off.

Flower 2 (8 petals)

Using red yarn, make 8 ch then join with a sl st into a ring.

Round 1: 1 ch, work 16 sc (UKdc) into the ring, join with a sl st to first ch.

Round 2: 1 ch, sc (UKdc) into same st as join, *1 ch, miss next sc (UKdc), sc (UKdc) into next ch, 8 ch, sc (UKdc) into same st,* repeat from * to * 6 times more, 1 ch, sc (UKdc) into same st as the first sc (UKdc), 4 ch, tr (UKdtr) into first sc (UKdc) to join [8 loops made].

Round 3: 3 ch to count as first dc (UKtr), work 7 more dc (UKtr) into the same loop (around the post of the dc (UKtr) in round 2), 1 sc (UKdc) into the next 1 ch sp, *15 dc (UKtr) into the next 8 ch loop, 1 sc (UKdc) in the next 1ch sp,* repeat from * to * 6 times more, 7 dc (UKtr) into the first loop, join with a sl st to the top of beg 3 ch [8 petals made]. Break off red.

Round 4: join in gold with a sl st to beg of previous round, work 1 sc (UKdc) into each sc (UKdc) all around each petal, join with a sl st to beg of round. Fasten off.

Leaves (make 3)

Using green yarn, make 13 ch.

Work 1 sc (UKdc) into 2nd ch from hook, 1 hdc
(UKhtr) into each of next 2 ch, 1 dc (UKtr) into
each of next 2 ch, 1 tr (UKdtr) into each of next
2 ch, 1 dc (UKtr) into each of next 2 ch, 1 hdc
(UKhtr) into next 2 ch, 1 sc (UKdc) into last ch.
Make 1 ch, now work along the other side of
the foundation in the same way, join with a sl st.

To make up

Work in the ends neatly on all the pieces. Take
a wire stamen and spread the beads into a flat
shape. Insert it through the centre of a flower,
twist the wire into a neat coil at the back of the
flower and secure with some firm stitches using
a needle and red thread. Repeat with the
other flower.

To make a bow

Cut the red ribbon into three 30cm (12in)
lengths. Find the points 7.5cm (3in) from each
end of the first length. Pinch the ribbon at
these points and bring the pinches together.
Squash the ribbon loop between the pinched
folds so it is flat and centred at the folds.
Repeat with the other ribbon lengths. When
you are satisfied with the result, assemble the
bows then take some fine wire and twist it
tightly around the centre. Arrange the loops
and tails of the ribbon in a pleasing manner
then trim the tails if desired. Arrange the
flowers and leaves on to the centre of the
ribbon, pin in position and then sew in place.

Acknowledgements

Many thanks to all the people involved in making this book possible. Thank you Search Press for your help and guidance, your fantastic photography and wonderful editing skills. Special thanks go to Cara Ackerman and DMC for supplying the fantastic array of Petra Yarns used to create all the projects in this book. And last but not least, thank you to my wonderful family and friends whose patience, help, understanding and encouragement are never ending.

Publisher's Note

If you would like more information about crocheting, try the *Beginner's Guide to Crochet* by Pauline Turner, Search Press, 2005.